For _____

From _____

Date _____

*I am my love's and my love is
mine. ~ Song of Songs 6:3*

BIBLE
PROMISES
for Newlyweds

BIBLE
PROMISES
for Newlyweds

PUBLISHING GROUP

www.BHPublishingGroup.com

NASHVILLE, TENNESSEE

Written and compiled by Karen Moore

Copyright © 2014 by B&H Publishing Group

All rights reserved

Printed in China

ISBN: 978-1-4336-8366-4

Published by B&H Publishing Group,
Nashville, Tennessee

Dewey Decimal Classification: 306.81

Subject Heading: MARRIAGE \ BIBLE—PROMISES \
DOMESTIC RELATIONS

Quotes taken from: *The New Encyclopedia of Christian
Quotations*, published by Baker Books, ©2000 John Hunt
Publishing Ltd. P.O. Box 6287, Grand Rapids, MI 49516-6287
and *The Complete Guide to Christian Quotations*, ©2011 Barbour
Publishing,Inc. P.O. Box 719 Uhrichsville, Ohio 44683

1 2 3 4 5 6 7 8 • 18 17 16 15 14

CONTENTS

INTRODUCTION

Arise, my darling. Come away, my beautiful one. For now the winter is past the rain has ended and gone away. The blossoms appear in the countryside. The time of singing has come, and the turtledove's cooing is heard in our land. The fig tree ripens its figs; the blossoming vines give off their fragrance. Arise, my darling. Come away, my beautiful one.
~ Song of Songs 2.11–13

It's hard to imagine a more romantic or beautiful picture of love than the one so poetically written in this Scripture from the Song of Songs. What can be more enticing than a beautiful bride to her groom, or the love shared between newlyweds?

Everything about life holds more promise and seems more alive with the fragrance of love. Colors are more vibrant throughout all of nature. Flowers are blossoming and birds are singing simply to honor the love of two people who have pledged to love each other for a lifetime.

Surely the winter of past loneliness has melted away and showers of sadness have turned only to rays of sunshine. If it all seems like coincidence, it isn't. It's totally by design. Just as you made promises to love for always, God long ago promised to love you forever. He embraces your new life as a couple and seeks to help you grow to become even more than you can imagine to each other. God promises to hold you up when difficulties arise and to offer you guidance as you seek Him.

This is your opportunity to strengthen your bond of love for one another and for Jesus Christ in the days and years ahead. Just as you stood at the altar and whispered vows to say "I do," now you stand together with Christ to design your marriage in such a powerful way that nothing on earth could ever unravel your three-fold cord. You have each other! You have God's love! What a wonderful way to start a brand new life!

Blessings to you both always!
Karen Moore

CHAPTER ONE

FROM ONE TO TWO,
AND TWO TO ONE!

Young husbands should say to their wives: I have taken you
in my arms, and I love you, and I prefer you to my life itself.
For the present life is nothing and my most ardent dream is
to spend it with you in such a way, that we may be assured
of not being separated, in the life reserved for us. I place your
love above all things, and nothing would be more bitter or
painful to me than to be of a different mind than you.
~ John Chrysostom

Just a short time ago, you were an individual who
had your own style, your own place to live, your own
work, and your own ambitions and desires. Now, you're
a newlywed, and you're learning what it means to be a

couple. You've shifted from being just one, to being two. Somehow, in the miracle that marriage brings, you'll shift again from being two to becoming one. As one, you'll walk arm in arm through life with the guidance of God.

Since this is the beginning of your marriage you get to define what it looks like and how you'll nurture and grow your relationship. The beautiful thing to know is that the promises you made to each other are reinforced by God's promises to be with you in all the events of your life from here. His pledge is to strengthen you with His love from this day forward.

It's Not Good to Be Alone

> Then the Lord God said, "It is not good for the man to be alone. I will make a helper who is like him." ~ Genesis 2:18

Honor Your Marriage

> Marriage must be respected by all, and the marriage bed kept undefiled, because God will judge immoral people and adulterers. ~ Hebrews 13:4

Stay Close Together

When a man takes a bride, he must not go out with the army or be liable for any duty. He is free to stay at home for one year, so that he can bring joy to the wife he has married. ~ Deuteronomy 24:5

I'm Yours, You're Mine!

I am my love's and my love is mine; he feeds among the lilies. ~ Song of Songs 6:3

Finding a Wife Is a Good Thing!

A man who finds a wife finds a good thing and obtains favor from the LORD. ~ Proverbs 18:22

Carry Each Other's Burdens

Carry one another's burdens; in this way you will fulfill the law of Christ. ~ Galatians 6:2

When Two Become One

"Haven't you read," He replied, "that He who created them in the beginning made them male and female," and He also said, "For this reason a man will leave his father and mother and be joined to his wife, and the two will become one flesh? So they are no longer two, but one flesh. Therefore what God has joined together, let no one separate." ~ Matthew 19:4–6

Give to Each Other

A husband should fulfill his marital duty to his wife, and likewise a wife to her husband. ~ 1 Corinthians 7:3

Stay Committed to Your Love

Wives, submit to your own husbands as to the Lord, for the husband is the head of the wife as also Christ is the head of the church. He is the Savior of the body. Now as the church submits to Christ, so wives should submit to their husbands in everything. Husbands, love your wives, just as also Christ loved the church and gave Himself for her to make her holy, cleansing her with the washing of water by the word. He did this to present the church to Himself in splendor, without spot or wrinkle or anything like that, but holy and blameless. In the same way, husbands are to love their wives as their own bodies. He who loves his wife loves himself. ~ Ephesians 5:22–28

Quotes and Sayings

Be the mate God designed you to be.
~ Anthony T. Evans

Love is the fulfillment of all our works.
There is the goal; that is why we run:
we run toward it, and once we reach it,
in it we shall find rest. ~ Augustine of Hippo

Love does not die easily. It is a living thing. It thrives in the face of all life's hazards, save one—neglect.
~ James D. Bryden

The way to love anything is to realize that it might be lost. ~ G. K. Chesterton

The most precious possession that ever comes to a person in this world, is the realization that you have won someone's heart. ~ Adapted from Josiah G. Holland

I have many reasons to make me love thee, whereof I will name two, first because thou lovest God, and secondly because that thou lovest me.
~ Margaret Winthrop

Prayer

Dear Lord, as we start our lives together, be in our midst. Be our Guide and our Companion, reminding us of the little things we can do for each other to strengthen our union. Bless our efforts to talk and listen with full hearts and attention to each other. Help us to always come to You when anything presents itself that seems too big for us to handle on our own. Thank You for bringing us together. Amen.

CHAPTER TWO

LEARNING TO SHARE AND PLAY TOGETHER

You cannot shortcut the growth process God has set up. You must "leave" home in a healthy way if you are ever to attain a fulfilling marriage relationship. ~ John Trent

You may think that "leaving home," whether it be you are leaving your parents' home or a home you've lived in on your own, will be an easy process. After all, you're in love and getting to live together is what you've planned for a long time. It may not be as easy as it sounds though.

Your old home had its familiarity, its predictable routines and comforts. You knew exactly who you were there, what role you had to play. As a newlywed, you're starting from scratch again. You're learning how to make a home with someone else. That means learning to share and play together in whole new ways. Be sure to invite God in to your new home.

Build a Strong House

> A house is built by wisdom, and it is established by understanding; by knowledge the rooms are filled with every precious and beautiful treasure. ~ Proverbs 24:3–4

Lift Each Other Up

> Two are better than one because they have a good reward for their efforts. For if either falls, his companion can lift him up; but pity the one who falls without another to lift him up. Also, if two lie down together, they can keep warm, but how can one person alone keep warm? And if somebody overpowers one person, two can resist him. A cord of three strands is not easily broken.
> ~ Ecclesiastes 4:9–12

A Tip for Husbands

Husbands, in the same way, live with your wives with an understanding of their weaker nature yet showing them honor as coheirs of the grace of life, so that your prayers will not be hindered. ~ 1 Peter 3:7

Strengthen Your Faith Together

For this very reason, make every effort to supplement your faith with goodness, goodness with knowledge, knowledge with self-control, self-control with endurance, endurance with godliness, godliness with brotherly affection, and brotherly affection with love. ~ 2 Peter 1:5–7

Beginning of Blessing

The vine, the fig, the pomegranate, and the olive tree have not yet produced. But from this day on I will bless you. ~ Haggai 2:19

Thank God for Your Future Together

LORD, You are my portion and my cup
of blessing; You hold my future. The
boundary lines have fallen for me in
pleasant places; indeed, I have a beautiful
inheritance. ~ Psalm 16:5–6

Be as One in the Lord

Walk worthy of the calling you have
received, with all humility and gentleness,
with patience, accepting one another in
love, diligently keeping the unity of the
Spirit with the peace that binds us. There is
one body and one Spirit—just as you were
called to one hope at your calling—one
Lord, one faith, one baptism, one God and
Father of all, who is above all and through
all and in all. ~ Ephesians 4:1–6

Apologize Quickly

Don't let the sun go down on your anger,
and don't give the Devil an opportunity.
~ Ephesians 4:26–27

Be Content with What You Have

I know both how to have a little, and I know how to have a lot. In any and all circumstances I have learned the secret of being content—whether well fed or hungry, whether in abundance or in need. I am able to do all things through Him who strengthens me. ~ Philippians 4:12–13

Put on Love

Above all, put on love—the perfect bond of unity. And let the peace of the Messiah, to which you were called in one body, control your hearts. Be thankful. ~ Colossians 3:14–15

Quotes and Sayings

God intended marriage for the mutual society, help and comfort that the one ought to have of the other both in prosperity and adversity.
~ The Book of Common Prayer

The marital love is a thing pure as light, sacred as a temple, lasting as the world. ~ Jeremy Taylor

Marriage was ordained for a remedy and to increase the world and for the man to help the woman and the woman the man, with all love and kindness.
~ William Tyndale

Laughter is the shortest distance between two people.
~ Victor Borge

Always laugh when you can; it is cheap medicine. Merriment is a philosophy not well understood. It is the sunny side of existence. ~ Lord Byron

Laughter can relieve tension,
soothe the pain of disappointment, and strengthen the
spirit for the formidable tasks that always lie ahead.
~ Dwight D. Eisenhower

prayer

Dear Lord, Help us to learn to live and play together in ways that please You and that will sustain our marriage. Help us to lighten up when we need to simply stop trying too hard and just laugh and hug each other. Help us to always keep the hopes and dreams of each other alive and well. Strengthen our love for each other and for You with each passing day. Amen.

CHAPTER THREE

SHARING YOUR FAITH AND YOUR PRAYERS

How sweet Your word is to my taste—sweeter than honey to my mouth. I gain understanding from Your precepts; therefore, I hate every false way. Your word is a lamp for my feet and a light on my path. I have solemnly sworn to keep Your righteous judgments. ~ Psalm 119:103–106

As a newlywed couple, you are now in the ultimate relationship, enjoying a commitment and communion that you will not have anywhere else. That means that each day of your marriage, you'll be consciously learning about each other and you'll be discovering more of who you both are in your relationship to God.

As you grow together, one of the things that will fortify you and strengthen your bond is your willingness and your ability to share your faith and to pray together. Beliefs are personal, but as a couple, you'll want to share your beliefs in ways that help each of you to gain new perspective on what God wants for your lives. What does it take? It takes communication, the same major ingredient you both need to keep your marriage strong.

God is always ready to communicate with you and He looks forward to the time you'll spend together. The words you share will be sweet to all of you.

Connecting to God

> I call with all my heart; answer me, LORD. I will obey Your statutes. I call to You; save me, and I will keep Your decrees. I rise before dawn and cry out for help; I put my hope in Your word. I am awake through each watch of the night to meditate on Your promise. In keeping with Your faithful love, hear my voice. ~ Psalm 119:145–149

Trusting Scripture

> All Scripture is inspired by God and is profitable for teaching, for rebuking, for

correcting, for training in righteousness,
so that the man of God may be complete,
equipped for every good work.
~ 2 Timothy 3:16–17

God Chose You

Therefore, God's chosen ones, holy and
loved, put on heartfelt compassion, kindness, humility, gentleness, and patience,
accepting one another and forgiving one
another if anyone has a complaint against
another. Just as the Lord has forgiven
you, so you must also forgive.
~ Colossians 3:12–13

It's Good to Ask

"Keep asking, and it will be given to you.
Keep searching, and you will find. Keep
knocking, and the door will be opened
to you. For everyone who asks receives,
and the one who searches finds, and to
the one who knocks, the door will be
opened." ~ Matthew 7:7–8

When You Don't Know What to Pray

In the same way the Spirit also joins to
help in our weakness, because we do
not know what to pray for as we should,
but the Spirit Himself intercedes for us
with unspoken groanings. And He who
searches the heart knows the Spirit's
mind-set, because He intercedes for the
saints according to the will of God.
~ Romans 8:26–27

A Fervent Prayer for You

For this reason I kneel before the Father
from whom every family in heaven and
on earth is named. I pray that He may
grant you, according to the riches of His
glory, to be strengthened with power
in the inner man through His Spirit,
and that the Messiah may dwell in your
hearts through faith. I pray that you,
being rooted and firmly established in
love, may be able to comprehend with all
the saints what is the length and width,
height and depth of God's love, and to
know the Messiah's love that surpasses

knowledge, so you may be filled with all the fullness of God.

Now to Him who is able to do above and beyond all that we ask or think according to the power that works in us—to Him be glory in the church and in Christ Jesus to all generations, forever and ever. Amen. ~ Ephesians 3:14–21

Love and Respect

This mystery is profound, but I am talking about Christ and the church. To sum up, each one of you is to love his wife as himself, and the wife is to respect her husband. ~ Ephesians 5:32–33

You'll Find Me When You Seek Me

"You will call to Me and come and pray to Me, and I will listen to you. You will seek Me and fine Me when you search for Me with all your heart. I will be found by you"—this is the Lord's declaration—"and I will restore your fortunes." ~ Jeremiah 29:12–14

Pray for One Another

Therefore, confess your sins to one another and pray for one another, so that you may be healed. The urgent request of the righteous person is very powerful in its effect. ~ James 5:16

Quotes and Sayings

The time to get your spiritual instrument in tune is early in the morning before the concert of the day begins. ~ Author Unknown

What can be more excellent than prayer; what is more profitable to our life; what sweeter to our souls; what more sublime, in the course of our whole life, than the practice of prayer! ~ Augustine of Hippo

*Let prayer by yourself alone, (or with your partner)
take place before the collective prayer of the family.
If possible let it be first, before any work of the day.*
~ Richard Baxter

*If you are swept off your feet, it's time to get
on your knees. ~ Fred Beck*

*Prayer is a sincere, sensible, affectionate pouring out
of the soul to God, through Christ in the strength and
assistance of the Spirit, for such things as God has
promised. ~ John Bunyan*

*Do not forget prayer. Every time you pray, if your
prayer is sincere, there will be new feeling and new
meaning in it, which will give you fresh courage.*
~ Fyodor Dostoevsky

Your vows were about a commitment to become one in the sight of God and your relationship will thrive the more you treat each other with love and respect. Value and appreciate your life together above all things and your marriage will last a lifetime. You will always be glad you made such an amazing commitment.

God promised to be with you on the day you made those vows, and learning to work together as a team of two will give Him the opportunity to walk with you each day. Your love for each other and your love for Him make all the difference. Your commitment is strengthened by a three-fold cord.

Faithful Love

> But He lifts the needy out of their suffer-
> ing and makes their families multiply like
> flocks. The upright see it and rejoice, and
> all injustice shuts its mouth. Let whoever
> is wise pay attention to these things and
> consider the LORD's acts of faithful love.
> ~ Psalm 107:41–43

Nothing Will Separate You from Me

Do not persuade me to leave you or go
back and not follow you. For wherever
you go, I will go, and wherever you live,
I will live; your people will be my people,
and your God will be my God. Where
you die, I will die, and there I will be
buried. May Yahweh punish me, and do
so severely, if anything but death separates you and me. ~ Ruth 1:16–17

Abiding Love

"Love the Lord your God with all your
heart, with all your soul, and with all your
mind. This is the greatest and most important command. The second is like it: Love
your neighbor as yourself. All the Law and
the Prophets depend on these two commands." ~ Matthew 22:37

A Married Man's Priorities

An unmarried man is concerned about
the things of the Lord—how he may

please the Lord. But a married man is concerned about the things of the world—how he may please his wife—and his interests are divided.
~ 1 Corinthians 7:32–34

No Separation from Christ

Who can separate us from the love of Christ? Can affliction or anguish or persecution or famine or nakedness or danger or sword? ~ Romans 8:35

God's Commitment to You

For I am persuaded that not even death or life, angels or rulers, things present or things to come, hostile powers, height or depth, or any other created thing will have the power to separate us from the love of God that is in Christ Jesus our Lord! ~ Romans 8:38–39

Your Commitment to God

As for me and my family, we will worship
Yahweh. ~ Joshua 24:15

Loyalty

Love the LORD, all His faithful ones. The
LORD protects the loyal, but fully repays
the arrogant. Be strong and courageous,
all you who put your hope in the LORD.
~ Psalm 31:23–24

Trusting God

For the word of the LORD is right, and all
His work is trustworthy. He loves righteousness and justice; the earth is full of
the LORD's unfailing love. ~ Psalm 33:4–5

Marriage Fidelity

Marriage must be respected by all, and
the marriage bed kept undefiled, because

God will judge immoral people and adulterers. ~ Hebrews 13:4

Quotes and Sayings

*Our loyalty is due not to our species but to God . . .
it is spiritual, not biological, kinship that counts.
~ C. S. Lewis*

*Unless commitment is made, there are only promises
and hopes . . . but no plans. ~ Peter Drucker*

*True and living devotion presupposes the love of God.
~ Francis de Sales*

Nothing is more noble, nothing more venerable, than fidelity. Faithfulness and truth are the most sacred excellencies and endowments of the human mind.
~ Cicero

Faithfulness is carrying out present duties in the best preparation for the future. ~ Francois Fenelon

The marital love is a thing pure as light, sacred as a temple, lasting as the world. -- Jeremy Taylor

Call nothing your own, but let everything be yours in common. ~ Augustine of Hippo

prayer

Lord, bless our marriage and help us to be always faithful to You and to each other. Let us seek to grow together and to commit ourselves always to our relationship. Guide us as we make decisions and choices that impact our lives as a couple. Give us grace to listen to each other's views and to strive for peace and joy in our home. Help us to always be committed to creating the best marriage possible. Amen.

CHAPTER FIVE

TALK, LISTEN,
LISTEN AND TALK!

Your speech should always be gracious, seasoned with salt,
so that you may know how you should answer each person.
~ Colossians 4:6

You've already learned about the benefits of talking things out, and listening with your hearts. A significant aspect of your relationship has been about discovering the most effective ways to communicate about everything.

You may have already discovered the things that cause your communications to fall apart. You may have had to develop some rules or tools you can use when it's hard to talk to each other.

God wants you to always talk to Him and strengthen your skills to be able to talk to each other about little things and big things. Any good relationship requires a speaker and a listener and there's a definite skill in being either and both.

As you both learn to listen and to speak with God, you'll build your foundation with each other by communicating all your needs and desires. Talk, listen, talk, and listen some more! It's a great way to continue to learn about each other and to build a strong relationship that will last forever. When in doubt, give God the last word!

Heartfelt Compassion

> Therefore, God's chosen ones, holy and loved, put on heartfelt compassion, kindness, humility, gentleness, and patience, accepting one another and forgiving one another if anyone has a complaint against another. Just as the Lord has forgiven you, so also you must forgive. Above all, put on love—the perfect bond of unity.
> ~ Colossians 3:12–14

God Holds the Future

> LORD, You are my portion and my cup of blessing; You hold my future. The

boundary lines have fallen for me in pleasant places; indeed, I have a beautiful inheritance. I will praise the LORD who counsels me—even at night my conscience instructs me. I keep the LORD in mind always. Because He is at my right hand, I will not be shaken. ~ Psalm 16:5–8

Be Quick to Listen

Understand this: Everyone must be quick to hear, slow to speak, and slow to anger, for man's anger does not accomplish God's righteousness. ~ James 1:19–20

Speak the Truth

Since you put away lying, Speak the truth, each one to his neighbor, because we are members of one another. ~ Ephesians 4:25

Build Each Other Up

No foul language is to come from your mouth, but only what is good for building up someone in need, so that is gives grace to those who hear. ~ Ephesians 4:29

Love Each Other

"I give you a new command: Love one another. Just as I have loved you, you must also love one another." ~ John 13:34

Listen and Learn

A wise man will listen and increase his learning, and a discerning man will obtain guidance—for understanding a proverb or a parable, the words of the wise, and their riddles. ~ Proverbs 1:5–6

Ears to Listen

Anyone who has ears should listen!
~ Matthew 13:9

God Knows Your Heart

Search me, God, and know my heart; test
me and know my concerns. See if there is
any offensive way in me; lead me in the
everlasting way. ~ Psalm 139:23–24

Think Before You Speak

LORD, set up a guard for my mouth; keep
watch at the door of my lips. ~ Psalm
141:3

Heart Talk

"For the mouth speaks from the overflow
of the heart. A good man produces good
things from his storeroom of good, and
an evil man produces evil things from
his storeroom of evil. I tell you that on

the day of judgment people will have
to account for every careless word they
speak. For by your words you will be
acquitted, and by your words you will be
condemned." ~ Matthew 12:34–37

Apples of Gold

A word spoken at the right time is like
gold apples on a silver tray. ~ Proverbs
25:11

Quotes and Sayings

Whoever lives true life, will love true love.
~ Elizabeth Barrett Browning

Not only to say the right thing in the right place, but
far more difficult, to leave unsaid the wrong thing at
the tempting moment. ~ George Sala

Kind words can be short and easy to speak but their echoes are truly endless. ~ Mother Teresa

In conversation, humor is worth more than wit and easiness more than knowledge. ~ George Herbert

Handle them carefully, for words have more power than atom bombs. ~ Pearl Strachan

Suit the action to the word, the word to the action. ~ William Shakespeare

prayer

Lord, be with us in our daily conversations. Make us mindful of the things we say to each other and help us always to be truthful and kind. Forgive us when we speak unfairly and help us desire to talk through the things that concern us. Let love truly guide our communications on every level. Help us to be faithful in our willingness to share the things that are important to our hearts. Amen.

CHAPTER SIX

FIXING THE MESSES AND HANDLING THE CONFLICTS

If anyone thinks he is religious without controlling his tongue, then his religion is useless and he deceives himself. Pure and undefiled religion before our God and Father is this: to look after orphans and widows in their distress and to keep oneself unstained by the world. ~ *James 1:26–27*

No doubt, you've already learned some things about handling those moments when the two of you don't see eye to eye. Even successful dating requires that you learn how to manage the situations that aren't easy. Marriage adds a new dimension though and now your love for each other may require some new skills, some new levels of how you'll fix the messes.

41

It's odd because sometimes you don't even see the conflict coming. You don't realize that you have very different opinions on what color to paint the bedroom, or how you want to spend a vacation. The beautiful thing is that it's great to have different opinions. Your lives would be a bit boring if you thought the same way about everything.

The part God wants you to remember is that it's not about what you say when you're feeling challenged, it's about how you say it. You are responsible for your tongue, that is, the words that come out of your mouth. Part of your marriage will hinge on learning how to give and receive differences of opinion and even criticism. If your attitude is one that seeks to grow your relationship, you'll find a way to be respectful and loving when you disagree.

God is always there with you, even in the midst of potential conflict. Seek His wisdom when you need help walking through those places of disagreement.

Clear the Air Quickly

> Be angry and do not sin. Don't let the
> sun go down on your anger, and don't
> give the Devil an opportunity.
> ~ Ephesians 4:26–27

Don't Insult Each Other

All bitterness, anger and wrath, shouting
and slander must be removed from you,
along with all malice. And be kind and
compassionate to one another, forgiving
one another, just as God also forgave you
in Christ. ~ Ephesians 4:31–32

Learn How to Speak to Each Other

A gentle answer turns away anger, but
a harsh word stirs up wrath. ~ Proverbs
15:1

Think Before You Speak

The mind of the righteous person thinks
before answering, but the mouth of the
wicked blurts out evil things. ~ Proverbs
15:28

The Foolish and the Wise

> A fool gives full vent to his anger, but a wise man holds it in check. ~ Proverbs 29:11

Love Is Patient

> Love is patient; love is kind. Love does not envy, is not boastful, is not conceited, does not act improperly, is not selfish, is not provoked, and does not keep a record of wrongs. Love finds no joy in unrighteousness but rejoices in the truth. It bears all things, believes all things, hopes all things, endures all things.
> ~ 1 Corinthians 13:4–7

Build Your House

> A house is built by wisdom, and it is established by understanding; by knowledge the rooms are filled with every precious and beautiful treasure. ~ Proverbs 24:3–4

Stay United and Connected

> If a house is divided against itself, that house cannot stand. ~ Mark 3:25

Don't Nag Each Other

> Better to live on the corner of a roof than to share a house with a nagging wife. ~ Proverbs 21:9

Quotes and Sayings

If I see conflict as natural, neutral, normal, I may be able to see the difficulties we experience as tension in relationships and honest differences in perspective that can be worked through by caring about each other and confronting each other with truth expressed by love. ~ David Augsburger

Truth carries with it confrontation. Truth demands confrontation; loving confrontation, but confrontation nevertheless. If our reflex action is always accommodation regardless of the centrality of the truth involved, there is something wrong. ~ Francis Schaeffer

A smooth sea never made a skillful mariner, neither do uninterrupted prosperity and success qualify for usefulness and happiness. The storms of adversity, like those of the ocean, rouse the faculties, and excite the invention, prudence, skill and fortitude of the voyager. The martyrs of ancient times, in bracing their minds to outward calamities, acquired a loftiness of purpose and a moral heroism worth a lifetime of softness and security. ~ Author Unknown

Life appears to me too short to be spent in nursing animosity or registering wrong. ~ Charlotte Bronte

The best remedy for anger
is a little time for thought. ~ Seneca

Be not angry that you cannot make others as you wish
them to be, since you cannot make yourself as you wish
to be. ~ Thomas à Kempis

Discussion is an exchange of intelligence; argument is
an exchange of ignorance. ~ Author Unknown

Silence is the unbearable repartee ~ Charles Dickens

All married couples should learn the art of battle as they should learn the art of making love. Good battle is objective and honest—never vicious or cruel. Good battle is healthy and constructive, and brings to a marriage the principle of equal partnership.
~ Ann Landers

Let go of your attachment to being right, and suddenly your mind is more open. You're able to benefit from the unique viewpoints of others, without being crippled by your own judgment. ~ Ralph Marston

Prayer

Father, when we find ourselves in a situation where we don't agree with each other, help us to share our viewpoints in respectful and loving ways. Help us to value each other, more than we value our separate opinions. Help us to come to You first, even before we begin to speak about an issue and seek Your guidance in the best ways to settle things. Grant that we would seek truth and understanding in compassionate and loving ways. Amen.

CHAPTER SEVEN

DEALING WITH CHANGE AND GROWING TOGETHER

Rejoice. Become mature, be encouraged,
be of the same mind, be at peace,
and the God of love and peace will be with you.
Greet one another with a holy kiss.
~ 2 Corinthians 13:11–12

As a newlywed couple, you expect to grow and to change. You anticipate that life will present you with options, sometimes things that bring joy, like moving to a new location for a great job, or finding out that you will have a baby in the near future. Other times, you'll be forced to change because things are not working as well as you had hoped that they would. You'll discover a need for advice and perhaps even counseling to help you solve issues that have come into play that were unexpected.

Part of your journey together is about finding the best ways to facilitate change. You'll learn how to cope with the things that can serve to bring you closer together, or that can attempt to drive a wedge between you. In any changes that come, seek the new path together. Take your concerns and your joys to God and let Him help you find the opportunities that will strengthen your marriage.

Don't let change become scary because it can only serve you well if you embrace it and grow with it. God will always be there to help you.

Can You Change?

Can the Cushite change his skin, or a leopard his spots? If so, you might be able to do what is good. ~ Jeremiah 13:23

Embracing Change

To the weak I became weak, in order to win the weak. I have become all things to all people, so that I may by every possible means save some. Now I do all this because

of the gospel, that I may become a partner
in its benefits. ~ 1 Corinthians 9:22–23

Disappointing Change

But when I hoped for good, evil came;
when I looked for light, darkness came. I
am churning within and cannot rest; days
of suffering confront me. ~ Job 30:26–27

Change May Be a Blessing and a Curse

Look, today I set before you a blessing
and a curse: there will be a blessing, if
you obey the commands of the LORD
your God I am giving you today, and
a curse, if you do not obey the commands of the LORD your God and you
turn aside from the path I command you
today by following other gods you have
not known. When the LORD your God
brings you into the land you are entering
to possess, you are to proclaim the blessing at Mount Gerizim and the curse at
Mount Ebal. ~ Deuteronomy 11:26–29

Growing Up

When I was a child, I spoke like a child,
I thought like a child, I reasoned like a
child. When I became a man, I put aside
childish things. ~ 1 Corinthians 13:11

Asking God for Change

God, create a clean heart for me and
renew a steadfast spirit within me. Do
not banish me from Your presence or
take Your Holy Spirit from me. Restore
the joy of Your salvation to me, and give
me a willing spirit. Then I will teach the
rebellious Your ways, and sinners will
return to You. ~ Psalm 51:10–13

God Provides the Growth

I planted, Apollos watered, but God
gave the growth. So then neither the
one who plants nor the one who waters
is anything, but only God who gives the
growth. ~ 1 Corinthians 3:6–7

Steps to Change

A man's steps are established by the
LORD, and He takes pleasure in his way.
Though he falls, he will not be over-
whelmed, because the LORD holds his
hand. ~ Psalm 37:23–24

Praise God in Change

Sing to Yahweh, you His faithful ones,
and praise His holy name. For His anger
lasts only a moment, but His favor, a
lifetime. Weeping may spend the night,
but there is joy in the morning. ~ Psalm
30:4–5

Change and Renewal

Do not be conformed to this age, but
be transformed by the renewing of your
mind, so that you may discern what is the
good, pleasing, and perfect will of God.
~ Romans 12:2

Quotes and Sayings

Everybody is in favor of progress. It's the change they don't like. ~ Author Unknown

Change is not made without inconvenience, even from worse to better. ~ Richard Hooker

Those who never retract their opinions love themselves more than they love truth. ~ Joseph Joubert

Change is the law. And those who look only to the past or present are certain to miss the future. ~ John F. Kennedy

Lord, when we are wrong, make us willing to change.
And when we are right, make us easy to live with.
~ Peter Marshall

If we don't change, we don't grow. If we don't grow, we
are not really living. ~ Gail Sheehy

What you are must always displease you, if you would
attain that which you are not. ~ Augustine of Hippo

If you are looking for painless ways to grow toward each
other and toward maturity, call off the search.
~ J. Grant Howard

And if any sudden call should occur, which we are not prepared to meet, let us not apply to others, till we first seek Christ.~ Author Unknown

Prayer

Dear Lord,

Thank You for being the Author of change and the One who provides so well for our growth. Help us to seek You in any changes that may come into our lives and our marriage. Help us to always be willing to share our fears about any changes we face so that we can help each other through the process. More than anything, Lord, help us to trust and believe that You are walking with us each day and even going before us to pave the way for all that will come. Strengthen our marriage through any gifts of change and create and even greater bond between us. Amen.

CHAPTER EIGHT

WHEN TROUBLE LANDS
WITH A CAPITAL "T"

*Our lives last seventy years or, if we are strong, eighty years.
Even the best of them are struggle and sorrow; indeed, they
pass quickly and we fly away. Who understands the power
of Your anger? Your wrath matches the fear that is due
You. Teach us to number our days carefully so that we may
develop wisdom in our hearts. ~ Psalm 90:10–12*

As you start out in your married life together, it's
going to be hard to predict just what is ahead. God
encourages us to stick close to Him, leaning on Him
for all that we need and for the direction and purpose
of our lives. He works with us through the troubles that
come our way, helping us to navigate the waters of fear

or disappointment. He stretches out His hand and offers us a place of comfort and peace.

As you become more accustomed to putting your lives in His hands, He reminds you that it's good to be aware of each new day, to be fully present. Trouble may come in and try to distract you. It may land front and center and occupy space for a while. Whatever it does, remember that good things and difficult things are part of living and part of the journey for you both. The main difference between you and others you may know is that you know where to go when trouble lands. God is your refuge and strength and you can depend fully on Him.

Our Help and Our Shield

> Now the eye of the Lord is on those who fear Him—those who depend on His faithful love to deliver them from death and to keep them alive in famine. We wait for Yahweh; He is our help and shield. For our hearts rejoice in Him, because we trust in His holy name. May Your faithful love rest on us, Yahweh, for we put our hope in You. ~ Psalm 33:18–22

Taste and See the Lord Is Good

Taste and see that the LORD is good. How happy is the man who takes refuge in Him! You who are His holy ones, fear Yahweh, for those who fear Him lack nothing. Young lions lack food and go hungry, but those who seek the LORD will not lack any good thing. ~ Psalm 34:8–10

God Protects You

Many adversities come to the one who is righteous, but the LORD delivers him from them all. He protects all his bones; not one of them is broken. ~ Psalm 34:19–20

Avoiding Trouble

All a man's ways seem right to him, but the LORD evaluates the motives. Commit your activities to the LORD and your plans will be achieved. The LORD has prepared everything for His purpose. ~ Proverbs 16:2–4

Jonah's Prayer and Yours

I called to the LORD in my distress, and He answered me. I cried out for help in the belly of Sheol; You heard my voice. You threw me into the depths, into the heart of the seas, and the current overcame me. All Your breakers and Your billows swept over me. But I said: I have been banished from Your sight, yet I will look once more toward Your holy temple. ~ Jonah 2:2–4

Seek God First

But seek first the kingdom of God and His righteousness, and all these things will be provided for you. Therefore don't worry about tomorrow, because tomorrow will worry about itself. Each day has enough trouble of its own. ~ Matthew 6:33–34

God Is Your Rock!

The LORD is my rock, my fortress, and my deliverer, my God, my mountain where I seek refuge. My shield, the horn of my salvation, my stronghold, my refuge, and my Savior, You save me from violence. I called to the LORD, who is worthy of praise, and I was saved from my enemies. ~ 2 Samuel 22:2–4

When Trouble Has a Capital "T"

LORD, do not rebuke me in Your anger; do not discipline me in Your wrath. Be gracious to me, LORD, for I am weak; heal me, LORD, for my bones are shaking; my whole being is shaken with terror. And You, LORD—how long?

Turn, LORD! Rescue me; save me because of Your faithful love. ~ Psalm 6:1–4

SOS to God!

LORD, I seek refuge in You; let me never be disgraced. Save me by Your righteousness. Listen closely to me; rescue me quickly. Be a rock of refuge for me, a mountain fortress to save me. For You are my rock and my fortress; You lead

and guide me because of Your name.
~ Psalm 31:1–3

God's Shield

Every word of God is pure; He is a
shield to those who take refuge in Him.
~ Proverbs 30:5

Quotes and Sayings

*In times of trouble, remember that God is: Too kind to
be cruel, Too wise to make a mistake, and Too deep to
explain Himself. ~ Author Unknown*

*If you see ten troubles coming down the road,
you can be sure that nine will run into the ditch
before they reach you. ~ Calvin Coolidge*

We should never attempt to bear more than one kind of trouble at once. Some people bear three kinds—all they have had, all they have now, and all they expect to have. ~ Edward Everett Hale

Worry does not empty tomorrow of its sorrow; it empties today of its strength. ~ Author Unknown

Oh, how great peace and quietness would he possess who should cut off all vain anxiety and place all his confidence in God. ~ Thomas à Kempis

I am an old man and have known a great many troubles, but most of them have never happened. ~ Mark Twain

prayer

Lord, when trouble comes calling, helps us to call on You. Help us to put any anxieties we may have at Your feet. Inspire us to trust You for our good as it applies to our marriage, our finances, our families, and our friends. Give us the strength to move past the obstacles of trouble that present themselves to us and to wait patiently and confidently for Your guidance in all situations.

Thank You for always being there. Thank You for being our Rock and our Refuge, our Savior and Friend. Bless our home and keep us forever diligent in You. We ask this in the name of our beloved, Jesus. Amen.

CHAPTER NINE

ROMANCE AND THE LIFE DANCE

Some directions for maintaining love are as follows:
1. Choose a good spouse in the first place. A spouse who is
truly good and kind. Full of virtue and holiness to the Lord.
2. Don't marry till you are sure that you can love entirely.
3. Don't be too hasty, but know beforehand all the imperfec-
tions which may tempt you to despise your future mate.
~ Richard Baxter

Richard Baxter was an English Puritan and though he lived in the mid-1600s, his advice is still rather sound. After all, if love is going to last a lifetime, then there are some guidelines in choosing a spouse that make that a greater possibility.

You're probably pretty content with his first directive. After all, you chose a good spouse in the first place. Through the dating process you learned about each other's personalities and mannerisms. You learned about their virtues and vices. But Richard's second statement is a bit harder to comprehend. His advice to not marry until you can love "entirely," may seem a little hard to imagine. Or, is it? Of course as newlyweds, you do love each other entirely. The hope is that you'll still love each other entirely on your fiftieth anniversary.

Alas, his third statement might be the toughest of them all. Knowing your partners imperfections may be harder to face. At this phase of your relationship, nothing but perfection reigns. However, the more you're willing to love and live with each other's less than stellar qualities, the better are the odds that you'll be married for a very long time. So, live and love, give each other room to grow and keep the romance alive. Your relationship will thrive on a foundation of love.

Love and Kisses

> Oh, that he would kiss me with the kisses
> of his mouth! For your love is more
> delightful than wine. ~ Song of Songs 1:2

The Delight of Love

Sustain me with raisins; refresh me with
apricots, for I am lovesick. ~ Song of
Songs 2:5

The Groom to the Bride

How beautiful you are, my darling.
How very beautiful! Your eyes are doves.
~ Song of Songs 1:15

The Bride to the Groom

My love is fit and strong, notable among
ten thousand. His head is purest gold.
His hair is wavy and black as a raven.
His eyes are like doves beside streams of
water, washed in milk and set like jewels.
~ Song of Songs 5:10–12

The Seal of Love

Set me as a seal on your heart, as a seal
on your arm. For love is as strong as

death; ardent love is as unrelenting as Sheol. Love's flames are fiery flames— the fiercest of all. Mighty waters cannot extinguish love; rivers cannot sweep it away. ~ Song of Songs 8:6–7

The Command to Love

"This is My command: Love one another as I have loved you." ~ John 15:12

Real Love

Love must be without hypocrisy. Detest evil; cling to what is good. Show family affection to one another with brotherly love. Outdo one another in showing honor. ~ Romans 12:9–11

Defining Love

Love is patient; love is kind. Love does not envy, is not boastful, is not conceited, does not act improperly, is not selfish, is not provoked, and does not keep a record

of wrongs. Love finds no joy in unrigh-
teousness but rejoices in the truth. It
bears all things, believes all things, hopes
all things, endures all things. Love never
ends. ~ 1 Corinthians 13:4–8

Walk in Love

Therefore, be imitators of God, as dearly
loved children. And walk in love, as the
Messiah also loved us and gave Himself
for us, a sacrificial and fragrant offering
to God. ~ Ephesians 5:1–2

Look Out for Each Other's Welfare

And be kind and compassionate to one
another, forgiving one another, just as
God also forgave you in Christ.
~ Ephesians 4:32

Quotes and Sayings

People are renewed by love. As sinful desire ages them,
so love rejuvenates them. ~ Augustine of Hippo

Love is not blind; that is the last thing it is.
Love is bound; and the more it is bound
the less it is blind. ~ G. K. Chesterton

Love is the sum of all virtue, and love disposes
us to do good. ~ Jonathan Edwards

Love does not dominate; it cultivates. ~ Goethe

The most precious possession that ever comes to a man in this world is a woman's heart. ~ Josiah G. Holland

Love does not make the world go round. Love is what makes the ride worthwhile. ~ Franklin P. Jones

To love is to be vulnerable. ~ C. S. Lewis

prayer

Dear Lord, we are so grateful that you gave us each other "to have and to hold" forever and ever. We know how blessed we are to have this gift of love to share. Help us keep the romance alive for years to come. Help us keep each other number one, with only You as our guide. We know that love is fragile and must be tenderly cared for each day or it can wither and die. Help us both to be great caretakers of our love. Amen.

CHAPTER TEN

EXPRESSIONS OF LOVE

"Love the Lord your God with all your heart,
with all your soul, and with all your mind. This is the
greatest and most important command. The second is like it:
Love your neighbor as yourself." ~ Matthew 22:37-39

Marriage is perhaps the truest test of our willingness to practice the Golden Rule. The person who shares your home and your heart is the one you have the greatest desire to please so that you live together in peace.

Though the ideals of love remain strong in the early years of marriage, they can sometimes be lost as familiarity sets in and couples assume they know what they need to know about their partner. In his book, *The Five Love Languages*, Gary Chapman tried to help us understand that love may be expressed in different ways and that it's important to know what expressions of love really have meaning for your partner. As you seek to know each other more fully over the years, look to understand the actions that spur you each on to greater love. Love is a word with a variety of definitions and you each need to define it for yourselves so you can share it completely with each other.

Love Is Patient

A patient person shows great understanding, but a quick-tempered one promotes foolishness. ~ Proverbs 14:29

Words of Affirmation

Pleasant words are a honeycomb: sweet to the taste and health to the body. ~ Proverbs 16:24

Loving Words Overflow

For the mouth speaks from the overflow of the heart. ~ Matthew 12:34

The Good Wife

Who can find a capable wife? She is far more precious than jewels. The heart of her husband trusts in her, and he will not lack anything good. She rewards him with good, not evil, all the days of her life. ~ Proverbs 31:10–12

Forgiving Each Other

For if you forgive people their wrong-doing, your heavenly Father will forgive you as well. But if you don't forgive people, you Father will not forgive your wrongdoing. ~ Matthew 6:14–15

Blessing Each Other

See to it that no one repays evil for evil to anyone, but always pursue what is good for one another and for all. Rejoice always! Pray constantly. Give thanks in everything, for this is God's will for you in Christ Jesus. Don't stifle the Spirit. Don't despise prophecies, but test all

things. Hold on to what is good. Stay
away from every form of evil.
~ 1 Thessalonians 5:15–22

Gifts and Generosity

Every generous act and every perfect gift
is from above, coming down from the
Father of lights; with Him there is no
variation or shadow cast by turning.
~ James 1:17

A Royal Woman

A capable wife is her husband's crown,
but a wife who causes shame is like rot-
tenness to his bones. ~ Proverbs 12:4

Things to Think About Together

Whatever is true, whatever is honor-
able, whatever is just, whatever is pure,
whatever is lovely, whatever is commend-
able—if there is any moral excellence

and if there is any praise—dwell on these things. ~ Philippians 4:8

The Beauty of Words

A man takes joy in giving an answer; and a timely word—how good that is!
~ Proverbs 15:23

Quotes and Sayings

Suit the action to the word, the word to the action.
~ William Shakespeare

Affection is responsible for nine-tenths of whatever solid and durable happiness there is in our lives.
~ C. S. Lewis

*The most courageous decision you make each day is the
decision to be in a good mood. ~ Voltaire*

*The smallest good deed is better than the greatest
intention. ~ Author Unknown*

*Love's secret is always to be doing things for God,
and not to mind because they are such very little ones.
~ F. W. Faber*

*There should be as little merit in loving a woman for
her beauty, as a man for his prosperity, both being
equally subject to change. ~ Alexander Pope*

True and living devotion presupposes the love of God.
~ Francis de Sales

The best and most beautiful things in the world
cannot be seen or even touched. They must be felt
with the heart. ~ Helen Keller

prayer

Father, please bless us with the desire and the ability to communicate our love to each other in appropriate ways. Help us to seek to understand before we have a need to be understood. Grant that we would grow past our mistakes and forgive each other quickly, ready always to give love a chance to renew us. Open our eyes to see each other in ways that will help us each offer the best of love in all its beauty and sacred joy. Thank You for teaching us the blessings of love. Amen.

CHAPTER ELEVEN

A PINCH OF PROSPERITY AND FLIMSY FINANCES

Now the God of all grace, who called you to His eternal glory in Christ Jesus, will personally restore, establish, strengthen, and support you after you have suffered a little. The dominion belongs to Him forever. ~ 1 Peter 5:10–11

One of the aspects of any marriage that causes joy and grief resides in the whole arena of money. We seldom believe we have enough money because no matter what we do, there is always another bill waiting to be paid. Sure, we can be more frugal, stick to a budget, and be reasonable about spending, but the pressures that can come to your finances can be very difficult. Often times we feel that prosperity is just around the corner, but currently you are living on financial fumes.

As a couple, you need to set your own guidelines about the flow of money through your household. You need to help each other set the rules, so that you can agree on what your financial picture needs to look like. Having a back-up plan for what you'll do when there is more month than money is a good idea!

Is it extremely important that you invite God in your conversation about your finances, asking for wisdom and direction. He will help you build a good financial foundation.

What You Get

> "No one can receive a single thing
> unless it's given to him from heaven."
> ~ John 3:27

Getting Your Priorities Straight

> But seek first the kingdom of God and
> His righteousness, and all these things
> will be provided for you. Therefore don't
> worry about tomorrow, because tomor-
> row will worry about itself. Each day has
> enough trouble of its own. ~ Matthew
> 6:33–34

Know Your Calling

Then the trees said to the fig tree,
"Come and reign over us." But the fig
tree said to them, "Should I stop giving
my sweetness and my good fruit, and
rule over trees?"

Later, the trees said to the grapevine, "Come and reign over us." But the
grapevine said to them, "Should I stop
giving my wine that cheers both God
and man, and rule over trees?"
~ Judges 9:10–13

Prosperity and Adversity

In the day of prosperity be joyful, but in
the day of adversity, consider: God has
made the one as well as the other, so that
man cannot discover anything that will
come after him. ~ Ecclesiastes 7:14

The Difficulty of Money

The one who loves money is never
satisfied with money, and whoever loves
wealth is never satisfied with income.
This too is futile. When good things
increase, the ones who consume them
multiply; what, then, is the profit to the
owner, except to gaze at them with his
eyes? The sleep of the worker is sweet,
whether he eats little or much, but the
abundance of the rich permits him no
sleep. ~ Ecclesiastes 5:10–12

God Sees Your Financial Picture

The LORD is a refuge for the oppressed,
a refuge in times of trouble. Those who
know Your name trust in You because
You have not abandoned those who seek
You, Yahweh. ~ Psalm 9:9–10

The Source of Wealth

You may say to yourself, "My power and
my own ability have gained this wealth

for me," but remember that the LORD your God gives you the power to gain wealth, in order to confirm His covenant He swore to your fathers, as it is today.
~ Deuteronomy 8:17–18

God's Generosity

The LORD brings poverty and gives wealth; He humbles and He exalts. He raised the poor from the dust and lifts the needy from the garbage pile. He seats them with noblemen and gives them a throne of honor. For the foundations of the earth are the LORD's; He has set the world on them. ~ 1 Samuel 2:7–8

The Battle of Rich and Poor

One man pretends to be rich but has nothing; another pretends to be poor but has great wealth.

Riches are a ransom for a man's life, but a poor man hears no threat.
~ Proverbs 13:7–8

Real Treasures

"Don't collect for yourselves treasures on earth, where moth and rust destroy and where thieves break in and steal. But collect for yourselves treasures in heaven, where neither moth nor rust destroys, and where thieves don't break in and steal. For where your treasure is, there your heart will be also." ~ Matthew 6:19–21

Quotes and Sayings

There is nothing wrong with people possessing riches. The wrong comes when riches possess people.
~ Billy Graham

Prosperity is not without many fears and distastes; adversity not without many comforts and hopes.
~ Francis Bacon

*God often takes a course for accomplishing His purposes
directly contrary to what our narrow views would
prescribe. He brings a death upon our feelings, wishes
and prospects when He is about to give us the desire of
our hearts ~ John Newton*

*Christian, remember the goodness of God in
the frost of adversity. ~ C. H. Spurgeon*

*Our whole life is taken up with anxiety for personal
security, with preparations for living, so that we really
never live at all. ~ Tolstoy*

Take courage, and turn your troubles, which are without remedy, into material for spiritual progress. Often turn to our Lord, who is watching you, poor frail little being as you are, amid your labors and distractions. ~ Francis de Sales

The difficulties, hardships, and trials of life, the obstacles one encounters on the road to fortune, are positive blessings. They knit the muscles more firmly, and teach self-reliance. Peril is the element in which power is developed. ~ William Matthews

What then are we to do about our problems? We must learn to live with them until such time as God delivers us from them. We must pray for grace to endure them without murmuring. Problems patiently endured will work for our spiritual perfecting. They harm us only when we resist them or endure them unwillingly.
~ A. W. Tozer

Prayer

Lord, we thank You for all the blessings You have given us. As we begin our married life together, help us to always seek You first in the things that cause us difficulty. Whether we have financial woes or even have prosperous times, help us to keep our focus on the direction You want for us and to know that You are with us in both adversity and prosperity. Amen.

CHAPTER TWELVE

BALANCING FAMILIES, JOBS, AND DREAMS THAT GOT AWAY

Stop worrying about whether or not you're effective. Worry about what is possible for you to do, which is always greater than you imagine. ~ Archbishop Oscar Romero

When you first get married, it can be very difficult to balance outside distractions. When you committed yourself to this relationship, you also created numerous new relationships with others. Along with your partner, you now have a new extended family to get to know. That new family may or may not be one you can easily embrace.

When it was just you, you were able to work late and on weekends but now you have a spouse who needs your love and attention. Maybe you had a dream to do something that is more difficult to do together than when you were single.

As you grow into your new roles as married partners, some of these other aspects of life can cause issues you didn't have before and ones that are not always readily solved. They may well give you reason for lively discussions and fervent prayers. Recognizing that "all things work together for good," can help you get through those times. God promises to guide you and walk with you through every aspect of change, whether the changes are easy or difficult.

Wisdom for New Situations

"Whoever is inexperienced, enter here!"
To the one who lacks sense, she says,
"Come, eat my bread, and drink the wine
I have mixed. Leave inexperience behind,
and you will live; pursue the way of
understanding." ~ Proverbs 9:4 6

God Sees You

All a man's ways seem right to him, but
the LORD evaluates the motives. Doing

what is righteous and just is more accept-
able to the LORD than sacrifice.
~ Proverbs 21:2–3

Be Humble

Walk worthy of the calling you have
received, with all humility and gentleness, with patience, accepting one
another in love, diligently keeping the
unity of the Spirit with the peace that
binds us. ~ Ephesians 4:1–3

Inheriting the Blessing

For the one who wants to love life and to
see good days must keep his tongue from
evil and his lips from speaking deceit,
and he must turn away from evil and do
what is good. He must seek peace and
pursue it, because the eyes of the Lord
are on the righteous and His ears are
open to their request. ~ 1 Peter 3:10–12

The Practice of Loving Everyone

> Little children, we must not love with word or speech, but with truth and action. This is how we will know we belong to the truth and will convince our conscience in His presence, even if our conscience condemns us, that God is greater than our conscience, and He knows all things. ~ 1 John 3:18–20

A Little Mary, A Little Martha

> While they were traveling, He entered a village, and a woman named Martha welcomed Him into her home. She had a sister named Mary, who also sat at the Lord's feet and was listening to what He said. But Martha was distracted by her many tasks, and she came up and asked, "Lord, don't You care that my sister has left me to serve alone? So tell her to give me a hand."
>
> The Lord answered her, "Martha, Martha, you are worried and upset about many things, but one this is necessary.

Mary has made the right choice, and it will not be taken away from her." ~ Luke 10:38–42

A House Divided

"Every kingdom divided against itself is headed for destruction, and a house divided against itself falls." ~ Luke 11:17

Your Work

Therefore, dear brothers, be steadfast, immovable, always excelling in the Lord's work, knowing that your labor in the Lord is not in vain. ~ 1 Corinthians 15:58

Loving and Working

Seek to lead a quiet life, to mind your own business, and to work with your own hands, as we commanded you, so that you may walk properly in the presence of outsiders and not be dependent on anyone. ~ 1 Thessalonians 4:11–12

God's Blessing

May our Lord Jesus Christ Himself and
God our Father, who has loved us and
given us eternal encouragement and good
hope by grace, encourage your hearts and
strengthen you in every good work and
word. ·· 2 Thessalonians 2:16 17

Quotes and Sayings

*Everyone thinks of changing the world, but no one
thinks of changing himself. ~ Leo Tolstoy*

*Faced with the choice between changing one's mind and
proving there is no need to do so, almost everyone gets
busy on the proof. ~ John Kenneth Galbraith*

Lord, when we are wrong, make us willing to change.
And when we are right, make us easy to live with.
~ Peter Marshall

Character is better than ancestry, and personal conduct
is more important than the highest parentage.
~ Thomas Barnardo

Parents can only give good advice or put them on the
right paths, but the final forming of a person's character
lies in their own hands. ~ Anne Frank

The union of the family lies in love;
and love is the only reconciliation of authority
and liberty. ~ Robert Hugh Benson

*God is the first object of our love: Its next office is to
bear the defects of others. And we should begin the
practice of this amid our own household.* ~ John Wesley

*Pray together and read the Bible together. Nothing
strengthens a marriage and family more. Nothing is a
better defense against Satan.* ~ Billy Graham

Prayer

*Lord, we're going through a lot of changes. We're
learning to love each other's families, we're learning
to balance our work lives with our home life, and
we're learning to follow Your plans for our future.
Help us to trust Your direction and Your counsel.
Help us to respect each other's ideas and to honor each
other's families. Help us to move forward in joy in
every area of our lives. Amen.*

CHAPTER THIRTEEN

PLANNING FOR THE FUTURE

*Don't boast about tomorrow, for you don't know
what a day might bring. ~ Proverbs 27:1*

As a newly married couple, your lives are full of hopes and dreams about tomorrow. Before the wedding, you were all about plans and creating a beautiful memory. Don't stop now!

Imagine what it would be like if you took that same kind of energy and love and enthusiasm and put it into the next year of your lives together and the one after that, too. What if you eagerly put your lives in God's hands and walked with joy into the future, the future you dreamed would come true?

Of course, only God knows each step you'll take and each opportunity He wants you to embrace, but knowing that you are connected to His love and His desire for you makes your future more secure. Walk with Him, with joy, with dreams, and with hope because He will indeed always be with you.

God Holds Your Tomorrows

> But seek first the kingdom of God and His righteousness, and all these things will be provided for you. Therefore don't worry about tomorrow, because tomorrow will worry about itself. Each day has enough trouble of its own. ~ Matthew 6:33–34

Thinking About Tomorrow

> Come now, you who say, "Today or tomorrow we will travel to such and such a city and spend a year there and do business and make a profit." You don't even know what tomorrow will bring— what your life will be! For you are like

smoke that appears for a little while, then vanishes.

Instead, you should say, "If the Lord wills, we will live and do this or that." ~ James 4:13–15

Building Your House

Unless the LORD builds a house, its builders labor over it in vain; unless the LORD watches over a city, the watchman stays alert in vain. ~ Psalm 127:1

Experience

The inexperienced one believes anything, but the sensible watch his steps. ~ Proverbs 14:15

Your Need for Jesus

"I am the vine; you are the branches. The one who remains in Me and I in him produces much fruit, because you can do nothing without Me. If anyone does not

remain in Me, he is thrown aside like a
branch and he withers." ~ John 15:5–6

Following God

Follow the whole instruction the LORD
your God has commanded you, so that
you may live, prosper, and have a long
life in the land you will possess.
~ Deuteronomy 5:33

God Goes Before You

A man's steps are established by the
LORD, and He takes pleasure in his way.
Though he falls, he will not be over-
whelmed, because the LORD holds his
hand. ~ Psalm 37:23–24

Listen for the Lord's Guidance

Your eyes will see your Teacher, and
whenever you turn to the right or to the
left, your ears will hear this command

behind you: "This is the way. Walk in it."
~ Isaiah 30:20–21

What God Wants from You

He has told you men what is good and
what it is the LORD requires of you: to
act justly, to love faithfulness, and to walk
humbly with your God. ~ Micah 6:8

The Perfect Plan

We have also received an inheritance in
Him, predestined according to the purpose of the One who works out everything in agreement with the decision of
His will, so that we who had already put
our hope in the Messiah might bring
praise to His glory. ~ Ephesians 1:11–12

Quotes and Sayings

The future is as bright as the promises of God.
~ Adoniram Judson

I know not what the future hath
Of marvel or surprise;
Assured of this, that life and earth
His mercy underlies. ~ John Greenleaf Whittier

Planning is bringing the future into the present so you
can do something about it now. ~ Alan Lakein

The moment you wake up each morning, all your wishes and hopes for the day rush at you like wild animals. And the first job each morning consists in shoving it all back; in listening to that other voice, taking that other point of view, letting that other, larger, stronger, quieter life come flowing in. ~ C. S. Lewis

Coming together is a beginning; keeping together is progress; working together is success. ~ Henry Ford

God from eternity, decrees or permits all things that come to pass, and perpetually upholds, directs and governs all creatures and all events; yet so as not in any wise to be the author or approver of sin nor to destroy that free agency and responsibility of intelligent creatures. ~ James Boyce

And I said to the man who stood at the gate of the year: "Give me a light that I may tread safely into the unknown." And he replied: "Go out into the darkness and put your hand into the hand of God. That shall be to you better than light, and safer than a known way."
~ *Minnie L. Haskins*

Prayer

Lord, we trust You with our future. We know that You have a plan for our individual lives and for our marriage. Help us to seek Your guidance and put our hands into Yours so that we may step into the future knowing You lead the way. Remind us to pray about each step we want to take and to always seek You first in decisions we face. Bless our present and our future according to Your will and mercy. Amen.

Chapter Fourteen

In Gratitude and Praise

Rejoice always! Pray constantly! Give thanks in everything, for this is God's will for you in Christ Jesus.
~ 1 Thessalonians 5:16–18

It's probably not difficult for the two of you to come up with a lot of things to be thankful to God for . . . after all, He gave you each other and that's a wonderful thing! As you grow in your marriage relationship though, you're going to discover many more reasons to be grateful for each other and the gifts you bring to your everyday lives.

Other times, you may experience things in your relationship that are a little harder to praise God about. You'll have upsetting moments and family concerns.

You'll have job related stress and crazy neighbors. Life will start to intrude on your little nest and the two of you will have a lot of other battles to fight. The world will literally come into your house and try to take up residence.

One way to combat the world is to remember the advice from the writer of Thessalonians. Give thanks in everything! That doesn't mean you have to be grateful "for" everything, but that if you start with a heart of gratitude, you may get to resolution and understanding much more quickly whatever the situation is. Give praise when things confuse you. Give thanks when things are great! The same God hears you and comes to you with love when you thank Him for all you have.

Rejoice Today

> This is the day the LORD has made; let us rejoice and be glad in it. ~ Psalm 118:24

Give Thanks!

> Give thanks to the LORD, for He is good;
> His faithful love endures forever.
> ~ Psalm 118:1

Sing to the Lord

I will sing about the LORD's faithful love
forever; I will proclaim Your faithfulness
to all generations with my mouth. For
I will declare, "Faithful love is built up
forever; You establish Your faithfulness in
the heavens." ~ Psalm 89:1–2

It Is Good to Praise the Lord

It is good to praise Yahweh, to sing praise
to Your name, Most High, to declare
Your faithful love in the morning and
Your faithfulness at night, with a ten-
stringed harp and the music of a lyre.
   For You have made me rejoice, LORD,
by what You have done; I will shout for joy
because of the works of Your hands. How
magnificent are Your works, LORD, how
profound Your thoughts! ~ Psalm 92:1–5

Everyday Gratitude

Sing a new song to the LORD; sing to
the LORD, all the earth. Sing to Yahweh,

praise His name; proclaim His salvation from day to day. Declare His glory among the nations, His wonderful works among all peoples. For the LORD is great and is highly praised. ~ Psalm 96:1–4

A Little More Praise

Enter His gates with thanksgiving, and His courts with praise. Give thanks to Him and praise His name. For Yahweh is good, and His love is eternal; His faithfulness endures through all generations. ~ Psalm 100:4–5

Victory Thanks

But thanks be to God, who gives us the victory through our Lord Jesus Christ! ~ 1 Corinthians 15:57

Celebrate in Thanks

You will joyfully draw water from the springs of salvation, and on that day you will say; "Give thanks to Yahweh; proclaim His name! Celebrate His works among the peoples. Declare that His name is exalted. Sing to Yahweh for He has done glorious things. Let this be known throughout the earth." ~ Isaiah 12:3–5

Quotes and Sayings

Be on the lookout for mercies. The more we look for them, the more of them we will see. . . . Better to lose count while naming your blessings than to lose your blessings to counting your troubles. ~ Author Unknown

Two of the most important phrases in the world are, "Thank you," and "Forgive me." Say the first often in your lifetime and you will only need the second on your deathbed. ~ Author Unknown

*In ordinary life we hardly realize that we receive
a great deal more than we give, and that it is only
with gratitude that life becomes rich. It is very easy to
overestimate the importance of our own achievements
in comparison with what we owe others.
~ Dietrich Bonhoeffer*

*A thankful heart is not only the greatest virtue, but the
parent of all other virtues. ~ Cicero*

*Reflect on your present blessings—of which everyone
has many—not on your past misfortunes, of which
everyone has some. ~ Charles Dickens (adapted)*

*A single grateful thought raised to heaven is the most
perfect prayer. ~ Gotthold Ephraim Lessing*

We ought to give thanks for all fortune; if it is good, because it is good, if bad, because it works in us patience, humility and the contempt of this world and the hope of our eternal country. ~ C. S. Lewis

*Both, gratitude for God's past and current mercies, as well as hope-filled expectation of His future mercy are the strongest motives to live for His glory.
~ Scott Meadows*

*A life in thankfulness releases the glory of God.
~ Bengt Sundberg*

prayer

Dear Lord, we are indeed thankful to You for having given us so much already in our marriage. We thank You that we can take our cares and concerns to You. We thank You that You watch out for us and for our well-being. We thank You for knowing us so well and for preparing our hearts to know You and the work You would have us do. Help us always to remain full of humble thanks knowing that everything we have comes from Your gracious love and mercy. Amen.

CHAPTER FIFTEEN

FROM THIS DAY FORWARD . . . MORE GUIDANCE FOR LIVING

*Outdo one another in showing honor. Do not lack dili-
gence; be fervent in spirit; serve the Lord. Rejoice in hope;
be patient in affliction; be persistent in prayer. Share with
the saints in their needs; pursue hospitality. Bless those who
persecute you; bless and do not curse. Rejoice with those who
rejoice; weep with those who weep. Be in agreement with one
another. ~ Romans 12:10–16*

Whether you've been married for a few months
now or a few years, you're always "newlyweds" because
you're always going to be learning something new about
each other. Since life is all about growing and changing
and becoming even more of what God wanted you to

become, you may find these promises of God's love and faithfulness to be helpful through every stage and age of your married life. Remember that the greatest joy you have is in each other as long as you keep your marriage vows sacred and your priorities straight.

In ancient biblical cultures, warriors were not allowed to go into battle for one year after they married, so that they were sure to have time to establish the relationship with their bride. Today, of course, the work intervenes just moments after the honeymoon, demanding that you get back to work, back to reality, back to what life was like before. The problem is, that life isn't like it was before. It is new. You're new! You have a new responsibility and a new focus. Keep that focus strong and God will watch your marriage thrive and grow. You will always feel His blessing and His presence.

Count Your Daily Blessings

> Teach us to number our days carefully so that we may develop wisdom in our hearts. ~ Psalm 90:12

God's Gift to You

He Himself gives everyone life and breath and all things. From one man He has made every nationality to live over the whole earth and has determined their appointed times and the boundaries of where they live. He did this so they might seek God, and perhaps they might reach out and find Him, though He is not far from each one of us. For in Him we live and move and exist, as even some of your own poets have said, "For we are also His offspring." ~ Acts 17:25–28

Love One Another

Do not owe anyone anything, except to love one another, for the one who loves another has fulfilled the law. ~ Romans 13:8

Hope In the Scriptures

For whatever was written before was written in the past was written for our instruction, so that we may have hope through endurance and through the encouragement from the Scriptures. Now may the God of endurance and encouragement allow you to live in harmony with one another, according to the command of Christ Jesus, so that you may glorify the God and Father of our Lord Jesus Christ with a united mind and voice. ~ Romans 15:4–6

Advice for Prayer Time

Let your graciousness be known to everyone. The Lord is near. Don't worry about anything, but in everything, through prayer and petition with thanksgiving, let your requests be made known to God. And the peace of God, which surpasses every thought, will guard your hearts and your minds in Christ Jesus. ~ Philippians 4:5–7

Learning to Be Content

I have learned to be content in whatever circumstances I am. I know both how to have a little, and I know how to have a lot. In any and all circumstances I have learned the secret of being content—whether well fed or hungry, whether in abundance or in need. I am able to do all things through Him who strengthens me. ~ Philippians 4:11–13

Grow In Your Faith

But grow in the grace and knowledge of our Lord and Savior Jesus Christ. To Him be the glory both now and to the day of eternity. ~ 2 Peter 3:18

Hope Abounds

Now faith is the reality of what is hoped for, the proof of what is not seen. For by it our ancestors won God's approval by it. By faith we understand that the universe was created by God's command, so that what is seen has been made from things that are not visible. ~ Hebrews 11:1–3

Love Everlasting

For now we see indistinctly, as in a mirror, but then face to face. Now I know in part, but then I will know fully, as I am fully known. Now these three remain: faith, hope, and love. But the greatest of these is love. ~ 1 Corinthians 13:12–13

Quotes and Sayings

Humor is the great thing, the saving thing. The minute it crops up, all our irritations and resentments slip away and a sunny spirit takes their place. ~ *Mark Twain*

Hope is itself a species of happiness, and perhaps the chief happiness which this world affords. ~ *Samuel Johnson*

If you cannot exhibit true love at home, you cannot exhibit true love in marriage. ~ Max and Vivian Rice

When we fail to wait prayerfully for God's guidance and strength, we are saying with our actions if not our lips, that we do not need him. ~ Charles Hummel

Hang this question up in your houses—"What would Jesus do?" and then think of another—"How would Jesus do it?" For what Jesus would do, and how he would do it, may always stand as the best guide for us. ~ C. H. Spurgeon

Make everything as simple as possible, but not simpler. ~ Albert Einstein